THE PUBLIC SOUND

The Public Sound

Marina Lazzara

San Francisco, California

© 2021 Marina Lazzara

All rights reserved

ISBN-13: 978-1-7362624-6-7

Some of these poems appeared in one form or another in the following print or electronic literary magazines: *Amerarcana: The Bird and Beckett Review, Big Bell, Brooklyn Rail, Cape Cod Poetry Review, Dispatches from the Poetry War, ELDERLY, Jellyroll Magazine, and Milk & Cake Press.*

Cover artwork by Harry Bowden

Author photo by J. Lee

San Francisco, California

for poetry

CONTENTS

Great Wooly Wisdom	2
Winter Solstice	7
The Streetlights Are On Too Long At Night	8
Silence, A Whole	9
In Its Slant The Rhythmic Remembers	10
Paradise	11
Sun Dim Light	12
The Confidence of Motion	21
Tea Cup Ode	22
Dishes To The Creek	23
Deliberate Singing To A Day Moon	24
Your Wallet or Your Life	25
Roar of Hunters	26
The Weakness Of The Liver	27
Boarded Windows	28
In This Chair	29
Activity	30
Antique Clock Repair	32
The Public Sound Inside The Sun	37

GREAT WOOLY WISDOM

1.

Buckeye butterfly loops over the wall
A waterfall from the belly of a fig tree

Regardless of the weather
I memorize blue like algae

2.

People who pick up litter play it safe

The sun stirs the spotted accents of a breeze
Through my living room door, dust

What is dropped or thrown away
Something for your art

3.

Days really are gorgeous eggs
on the undersides of leaves

                (go drench) (go down)

"And to cleave to a semblance of motion.
Omniscience" *

Light is a manifesto

      and everything I just hang up
      which is not to be confused
      with silence

                Ted Berrigan: Sonnet 72

4.

If it were written, would it console you?

It's garbage night, trash day, clicking
        Something breaks

Yes, it would console me to have it written

To slowly stir the heated dairy forming skin

To crow perched like a bird crows

As if this wind were still

                a pulse

5.

Something breaks

    The masses sleep separately when they could melt

Tellima grandiflora beneath Sagebrush
Coastal Bluff blond and arid rushing over sand

    Just now the sound outside my window
    The now only odor of ash on the deck
    A long stretching bus wave
    The electric bar falls and a bus halts

    Bang of the middle night wakes
    The three coyotes in the park

    The raccoons grab the Sticky Monkey Flower
    The coming of the Great Wooly Wisdom

    I write poems, compost bins

WINTER SOLSTICE

the Raven this hour eats slanted winter light
        not some kundalini bird
                spilling a wing cut verse

Maizie's bird hides
        from noon sun in a mirror
one of the Earth's poles
        has its maximum tilt
toward the Sun
        reeling back in
a liquid eye, a stream

I want this day again
a dawn rendition
that won't die back

botanicals and public radio
when the rain comes that's it
soft sunset light
in the southwest

        off the false adobe sky

THE STREETLIGHTS ARE ON TOO LONG AT NIGHT

Today the hummingbird and I bump heads
My fault under black sage
   clearing oxalis, lifting to climb out
   a hummingbird and I run into each other
   my forehead, her beak
   and she hovers in front of me
   eye level and disgusted

Bang the purple flower of the black sage
Bang the sweet ash in my ear

Droughts bring flowers early and the ground
   hard pans and doesn't filter and the birds
   come out of their hover
   and show themselves more
   and so it is

searching for something dripping
she came down too low

Bang the purple flower of the black sage
Bang the sweet ash in my ear

SILENCE, A WHOLE

There seem breaks, lengths of silences which keep as distant the eyes making actual the whole of it.
                         Robert Creeley from *The Gold Diggers*

Silent Sycamore in the band shell courtyard

       sneak past those pollarding tools, sneak past

            those knobs like fists

Think of bowls on water in that fountain downtown

      splendid clicks, swish burrs
      as what's small in what we hear

Depth of pool   the turning and timing

Constant pool
Floating innards of boats
Placid as roads to wind
Dusk to dusk

Coyote walks across the courtyard
      orders a drink

Later, I watch my kid with that doll
      cuts her hair
      sits to dress her

          tangled yarn and tattered string

When eyes look into the sea
      the way you're looking at me, she says

that's called fake out

IN ITS SLANT THE RHYTHMIC REMEMBERS

      tree rings as constellations in my yard

The planter in thick garlic harvest
with few worms now an industry of castings

Place your astronomy right with that dirt
unlike accurate constellations
astonished by actual axis
a place shaped sea is wistful

moon rise, moon set and phase calendar for Palestine or Syria, April 2018
8:42 pm rising   moon passing 2:08
      10 great bars in Ramallah these days, cocktails more mellow on Thursdays

Read the stars   be home by now

      Everything brightly lit, possible travel

PARADISE

The other side is on fire
I seek out tiny dishes to place my ring on

The sky 'obscurium'   'obscurius'

In a book I read
By vapor of ointment, one levitates
Rich and discreet velvets, bird-colored
      Lost in night to misty scents

How quickly a zero tide evaporates

      Red tipped water plants
      Become land beasts

SUN DIM LIGHT

1.

I seal the secret of words five times
and get away with it

I slice the noon

2.

Organizing these stars into one bright dot of hot
white light
As simple as that

A puzzle is at hand for the eyes

There is no heaven unless we bury it

        Unmotivated fat horn
        Serenades branches in the park

3.

a nonsense best silent

        as far as rocks go

just best to plant

    feet firmly in the troubles

        of the earth, you say

narrate as it soothes

melancholy sovereignty

    weeps like a parable

a truant handheld sun

  the one like that lift

      all

        together

          now

      we're dying for

4.

The rower of a vast assembled boat

I launch the ship
        into the chaparral fires
Emergency systems turn off

Myths always have a golden tree

Stunt men and drugged boats
       dragging sands

              and paper birds for the dogs

5.

the words like pressed flowers

scream gorgeous, horrific laughter
      their shapes flattened for love

6.

The lid pops off the kettle and most of the water falls into a cup. Spread all over the linoleum, a geography of boxes and bottle caps. The heated steam. The rain pours down with distortion.

Not even the kids look up from their palms. Once witnesses to tiny people in the fields, their unreadable hand lines of fortune covered by device. The starlight is a book but the book is not a sun. Always trying to reconfigure, rewire, pronounce.

Swamp dredges the muck for lost vowels. Only letter after letter after dot after dot. Stuck in the mud.

Sun dim light down to love.

Look up to the sky
looks down
like a piece of paper.

7.

I turn the rain away

        pouncing on the page

in symphony for

        a sketch of the sun

a place the mile high

        Dracaena tips will burn

8.

the dream
into the delirium of awakening

I slice the noon and
the dead begin to move
beneath my feet

Slap stick cedar piles
switch to heavy
mirrors in the room

My wrists tire
I am older when we talk
    yellowing philodendron leaves

9.

Don't put the laptop on your knees
When the landline rings it's my mom

The kid is sick
Nothing knocks her out
She coughs with the rain
Record breaking kind of rain
        Flowering currants

These days there's no turning on
Turning off
Is where it's at
J. plugs in   I stand
In the wind of the amplifier
And get away with it for now

These days
        paper birds unfold from the dust
        that circles in the midriff of my room

I'm a looker outer

Dear David

6 drops of Yarrow for a slight fever. Sweat is a sign of cooling off
        but also of intense opening

                for David Meltzer, poet, teacher
                (Italicized line fragments from various Meltzer poems)

THE CONFIDENCE OF MOTION

What is it I keep forgetting, and why do I keep forgetting it
 T. Fortin from A Modern Champion of the World

What cunning fixture of day, mercurial

Indelible costume bent by gravity
       maybe fog, the inner ear

According to square roots & means
       Prisms become Pyramids

I'm standing on her doorstep
The middle of the Ocean
Holding my breath

Consciousness is a tricky little bugger
       very hard to kill

In the confidence
Of motion
       Equal of matter
       Equal in direction

       The way out or the way in
       Caesura

If I listen, I sense in tandem   with my own

       Her endless spiral, origins

for Annabelle Lazzara, my mother

TEA CUP ODE

Every shadow through a window plane
Feeling shadow though best feet are down

Above trees
Alder, Cedar, Monterey, Cypress

Juniper as a floor

In round rooms the white sky sucks height
To vertigo   a sound sculpture & a bird

      that hole in the floor

Whisper and you are whispered next to me
We are only here

We are turning into architecture
Or a tree, I'm not sure, I'm not sure

for Ava Koohbor

DISHES TO THE CREEK

toward the water

 soft wood

  from North

 a fork

and an entrance

move out of the way
get out of the way

soak soak soak

DELIBERATE SINGING TO A DAY MOON

Blossoms on a tree without leaves

    turn a wild space silouquet

shadowing for the solstice

    like a rock, like minds

In the breeze of the aired-out desert

    chewed up like a rattlesnake

        the swollen prey belly whole

            is excited for more

    to eat sorrow from the tapped out

        reasonings of the heart

        A hung jury

            Or a cup of water?

YOUR WALLET OR YOUR LIFE

We watch reports

    We don't knock down doors

Ask, have you seen the children

    Is my waking child with yours?

Has the thought of her in a crowded room
Stuck to save you in the know?

Sweet sleep smells in
    the constant dirt   gathering and amending

    the collapsed closet
    playing hide and see for a moment

        Being hidden as open

            concentrate   see

                being hidden as open

Bodies and tellings

        a raft with a stone

    A migrant and in sworn migration

        your wallet or your life

ROAR OF HUNTERS

Pawn a trick as animal calls, called
Animal as we are, call, call
House, hornet, filth
Rape & structure, just call it
   We are Animal
Playing funky not as is is face
Freedom toward the safari deal
Picky Picky Picky
Red moon over me talked meal
A boxing brew, this square written
Shaken for dinner
Whatever will heat up

I didn't know
        We were talking
                About a lion

Chomp Chomp Chomp

Rhododendron wine on the Himalayan trail
Twist slight sound   Record records in the dark
Stark
   Shark
Bark the roar of hunters

THE WEAKNESS OF THE LIVER

deep in night rain the windshield says to float

    it seems so easy to drift

        remain as viscosity to the curb

  emerge as

a sudden light

      a shadow puppet

  time submerged

yield a dandelion

      the last bit

    yields a last bit

      bends the streetlights

I bought another

    pet for my kid

after taking

several wrong turns

onto one-way streets

    in the Tenderloin

BOARDED WINDOWS

the street hills go up and then falling
over the hillside into algae filled ponds
ducks eat the green topping like oats

furthermore, the duck dancing is dinner

the people came first and then the boarded windows

I held this morning hints
of wrapping around this urban waist
my feet locked behind its back

my mother's neck sweat
sniffing sap, dripping

IN THIS CHAIR

Dolphins we won the other day in vision
and Maizie drinking sand by mistake as she sips

In this chair I am the pulling lift of the whirlwind
and the crystal mining long ago was long ago

rooted in shine

The plants have flowered enough
The bees are around still
I keep the flowering
long

In this chair I move my legs in variables
It sucks
No one gets the tapping
I have won

ACTIVITY

Really. We should
just drop

live with tents
the commons
find food
more telling
than the dropping

For what you
are is poverty

You think you
have anything more?

Politics of
the expecting
something
to find
what is a word
and the handling
of the broken blue
shade in on the wet
strip of lawn, four
feet long that's left
I can clean the bag
out for feeling
and dumpster dive
or be winged
and lie to you
about it
I'll grow so old
I'll grey
stay
awake all
night counting

ANTIQUE CLOCK REPAIR

1.

Hurry the night goes down
It's moody there going down

    Go
Get the ice back in me, get the cold
Movement in skates

Casting long sighs
Those seated around the table
Break hold to break bread and make
You be there
In a pot, starving in odor, like a pig
In hunger this way

I will feed you with my limb
If I have to
Break bone to feed you

2.

I've been looking for you
Bird or fish
This isn't my house but
I'm here like it's your house
Get rid of the rich with my swim
And make this flight shallow
What could be
Reeled, village fish
Urban fish
To feed you
Floating in currents backwards
With ear fin

3.

Four blocks down the hill
Bar owner says change
Is good for business
Rafters of birds
Move their flight with the shore
The fish move
Their scales with the swim

That grand collage   Poetry
On our backs, shifting loads

4.

Situate yourself.

Adjust your furniture

This manner in which we enter

Until we catch meteors for breakfast

Sun suffrage when everybody used to mingle

Used to body everybody

You, you thought I said finger not mingle

I think you know me

I think words set loose the lucid sea

THE PUBLIC SOUND INSIDE THE SUN

1.

Your original sigh, sucking and the active mind
A heart so unhinged thinking as it might, a shadow
On each word a shadow by far the light over the house tills
    You the ancient shadow murmuring hunger & intention

Their original intention
Fantasy ads and the four wheeled
Back roads to in seasoned foods

2.

Can't a baby just take a nap? Live in a house
like a Moroccan cap, green on red on orange? Ideal
to love this city September Sun with no worry
the pushy ground won't curtail.   How mellow
mossy photos down ride this feel, fall, flail, flap, fail

Can't a baby just cry?
        Somnambulist's weepy eye
Can't we stick her eye into our heads
and cry just once ourself some history?

3.

Some days the sky opens
in other places but the sky

I almost sleep without worry
the baby's cold

She sighs sometimes
like skin

The most sun on my face
is my neck & my name

The pebbles make a heart, she crawls
and moves in abundant sun

The slender yellow fan covering
the rounded buttocks of the Buddha-bent man in front of me is flat

Now is the time to gather acorns, walnuts
the Calyx opens to seed

Seasons skip succumb

4.

A breath in your head.   live with it

In the throat   in the moment

Catching up   no one's looking

Disturbed chord wonder

Baby, oh baby
Where will the fish be
When you shore gallop
In my dreams

5.

Everyone everywhere usually
Wants everything everyday mostly

6.

Beautiful you walk
a spider midair
my memory
    your father's eyes
Don't walk up that hill
Anemone hailing
    sea salt you wouldn't believe

7.

On Fell Street
    Quetzalcoatl
The Mexican Wind God
    the Bird
Feather headed
    & blowing
The baby from my arms

8.

Nettles, Alfalfa, Red Clover, Chamomile
Catnip, Echinacea, Fennel, Wild Oats
Ceonothus, Sticky Monkey
Live, Blue, White
    Oak
Miner's Lettuce, Shepherd's Purse
Chickweed   V I o let
Johnny Jump Up!
Calendula! Yarrow!
Salvias   *All Salvias*
Melissa officinalis
Vitex agnus-castus
Hypericum perferatum
Artemisia
Leonorus
Crataegus
Verbascus thapsus
Arctium, Rumex, Sassafras
Zingiber officinale
Sambucus, Thymus, Rosmarinus

    Cinnamomum
    Dandelion

9.

the economy   they say

oatmeal for hours on the stove
launders not swollen or over rocks
rodents & epidemics of books in the hall

living costs

10.

Take a bomb to the moon
Search water, condo credit, proper views

I'm not one affording a moon
vulnerable to be sighted as escape

our shared body
        water body

constellation's imprisoned coquette

11.

it is set in its perch
    the city midriff line
St. Ignatius, spied point hillside

taxi rides from South Van Ness, helicopter naps & black flags
on my corner Chevron, I think of Motherhood, secure my breast
what a privilege, a word I often misspell
eventually crawl out under radar

the tipsy trees froth winter
the tipsy trees froth winter

there are pharmaceuticals
in the water

12.

Keeping the blue jay occupied
found beneath a cup turned over, a sock that matches
my neighbor's shirt, a beautiful turquoise lake top
where the Sun corners off

Behind the Oak Woodlands
a blue jay landscapes the upper forest
the above cliff, hanging onto twigs
and somehow swinging with a hop to a pile

keeps the blue jay occupied
    as not to see new weather
once so shallow to speak of, winking

    Rhythmic running in the acorn corridor

13.

There are plastics sinking and fumes float
and assaults on pollination escape

There are keyboards as small mountains
where in China young boys search out silver

There are dark orange clouds
The blinds are open and the hollow hum hums

Eclipse wonders and pink promoters
and historical fiction legends true and we let

The hunt gather honey in our bones
while the bees fade with the story of this light

14.

the rounded flight
    offers windedness
        getting back, a fallen
    voice, the public
        sound inside the sun
            recorded light

street sighs & no more
construction today, only this:

knowing to grow old now

        (Okay, go)

                for Maizie Jade, my daughter

Marina Lazzara, 2021

Marina Lazzara was born in Easton, Pennsylvania, where the Lehigh River flows into the Delaware. She attended Old Dominion University in Norfolk, VA and studied English literature, creative writing, and art history. She moved to San Francisco in 1989, and joined the New College of California community, earning a MA/MFA in poetics. She has also studied horticulture and Western Herbalism.

Lazzara was part of the editorial collective associated with *Processed World* magazine and the creative community that arose around San Francisco's Adobe Books. She organized street theater, poetry readings and music events, advocating for life without meaningless work, and in pursuit of creativity and joy.

She has published in various literary magazines and with Two Way Mirror Books, a press she founded and continues to lead. The title of the press is a shout out to her teacher, the poet David Meltzer, from his book by the same name. With poets Patrick James Dunagan and Nicholas James Whittington, she edited *Roots and Routes: Poetics at New College of California* (Vernon Press, 2020).

She is also a musician and songwriter, and is currently a vocalist and guitarist for the San Francisco band, The Rabbles. She teaches with the Community Living Campaign.

THE PAGE POETS SERIES

Number 1
Between First & Second Sleep by Tamsin Spencer Smith

Number 2
The Michaux Notebook by Micah Ballard

Number 3
Sketch of the Artist by Patrick James Dunagan

Number 4
Different Darknesses by Jason Morris

Number 5
Suspension of Mirrors by Mary Julia Klimenko

Number 6
The Rise & Fall of Johnny Volume by Garrett Caples

Number 7
Used with Permission by Charlie Pendergast

Number 8
Deconfliction by Katharine Harer

Number 9
Unlikely Saviors by Stan Stone

Number 10
Beauty Will Be Convulsive by Matt Gonzalez

Number 11
Displacement Geology by Tamsin Spencer Smith

Number 12
The Public Sound by Marina Lazzara

www.ingramcontent.com/pod-product-compliance
Lightning Source LLC
Chambersburg PA
CBHW032059040426
42449CB00007B/1135